Praise for *Sun-Soaked Shadows*

"*Sun-Soaked Shadows* so beautifully captures nature's healing balm in times of immense grief and sorrow. The landscapes *Sun-Soaked Shadows* paints wrap you in waves of deep intimacy with not only Hannah's memories but the collective weight of loss, and a pathway through the labyrinth of grief."

– Shannon Lujan, *Artist*

"With unapologetic, blunt and unwavering honesty, Hannah's writings succeed in opening your eyes. Vivid and exhilarating, the poetic verses in *Sun-Soaked Shadows* are teaching moments for one's heart, soul and mind. *Sun-Soaked Shadows* is a gift to the world. Brave literature from a super self-aware poet, taking you on a journey, as epic poetry should.*"*

– Fadi, *Author of Bending Serendipity*

"As a fellow Scorpio moon, Hannah took the words from my heart and made it into a masterful work of art. *Sun-Soaked Shadows* gently touches into the depth of our most sacred and tender emotions, weaving words that spark love, offer solace in moments of grief, and instill hope in the heart. Every poem is a testament to the enduring power of grief as art to touch the soul and inspire."

– Paola Ucelo, *Artist*

sun-soaked shadows

Copyright © 2023 by Hannah Alley
First published in the United States of America
by Amazon.

Thank you for purchasing this book and complying with copyright laws. The material found throughout this book is not to be copied, scanned, reprinted, or distributed without prior permission.

ISBN 9798857620571 (paperback)

@heyhannahalley
www.hannahalley.com

Cover art by Shannon Lugan
Book design by Leslie D'Ambrosio

*for the grieving,
may you find places for love to flow.*

Author's Note

This journey has been one of self-inquiry and exploration. After my mother's death, I was drowning in all that was rising within, demanding to be felt. Consumed with grief while the world continued to turn, I began a mourning practice that involved uninterrupted time in nature (mostly my backyard), a notebook and some sort of somatic practice. It was a safe container that, once opened, had a cascading effect in releasing what had been previously buried deep in my tissues.

What needs to be felt will sooner or later rise to the surface whether you're ready for it or not. These writings were pulled from journal entries during those sun-soaked mournings between the years 2017 and 2021. It's taken me a lot of courage and the nudge of a few incredible people to bring these entries into the light. *You know who you are, and I am grateful.*

I write in deep reverence for nature, my greatest teacher, and for my mother, the first home I ever knew. But I'm publishing this for my five-year-old self, who has the most tender love for life. She always dreamed of becoming an author, and these days I just want to make her proud.

Much like grief, this collection is raw, scattered and unfolding. Sometimes I felt all lowercase, so poems are all lowercase. It's different than my first book, *everywhere, and in my heart*, in that I show you my darkness. I invite you to receive me and these words with an open heart and sense of curiosity.

       waves of love,

       Hannah Alley

Contents

let your heart shatter	2
petrichor	4
velvet sea	5
last words	6
i.f.m.y.m.	8
our bones remember	15
dreams	16
immortality	20
she wolf	21
3am, again	22
god, is that you?	25
the smell of you	26
You are what the world needs	28
metamorphosis	30
wombyn	31
immersed	32
g is for grief	34
good time girl	36
coconino	37
middle of nowhere	38
the sweetness of time	39
wet soil & serpentine	40

undone with the one	42
w.i.p.	43
mystic in the mirror	44
pink bottom girls	45
supai, 2020	46
truth is weightless	49
more	50
sweet child of mine	51
kids can't be caged	52
benevolent	55
connected to the flow	56
mirrors	57
wakan	58
true unity	60
what if we gave the land back?	61
root wisdom	62
medicine prayers	63
dying to live	66
happy is in the details	68
a conversation with my shadow	72
winds of change	74
eclipse	75
queen of swords	76
a winding road is more fun to travel	78

try everything once, twice if you like it	80
damp thoughts	81
Scorpio moon	82
soul shine	83
red rocks	87
disaster on the inside	88
taking radical responsibility for my own healing	89
all the ways to love	90
don't pick the weeds	92
let me show you	93
love right under your nose	96
sun spirit	97
drops of devotion	98
fleshly desire	99
slow dance w/ death	100
let's free fall for a while	101
everywhere, and in my heart	102
Strange Love	105
When your Bones just Know	108
February	110
let's live, kid	111
spirit embodied	112
lonely	113
quantum birth	115
gratitude practice	119

the womb	120
jumping into the void	121
the town that made me	123
a lifetime of guilt	124
why do bad things happen to good people?	128
allow me to rise	132
the edge of identity	135
1000 lifetimes healed	136
becoming the one	139
who decides who is worthy of liberation?	140
Learning to Balance	142
woman in waiting	144
balancing act	145
character development	147
remembering who i am	148
Dave Matthews was right	151
what it does	152
On Choosing Life	154
rediscovering love after loss	158
2.2.22	160
aquarius	161
one in the same	162
august wisdom	165
sun-soaked shadows	166

sun-soaked shadows

thank you, sun
for casting
shadows
in them i'm
reminded
beauty exists
everywhere,
in all things.

// let your heart shatter

Let your heart shatter.

Watch as every piece of your grief-stricken heart falls to the floor. Be there wide open, raw, vulnerable, maybe shaking   with   fear.

In a vast unknown land of loss, naked in the dark, with your lonely bones scattered far and wide, it will feel impossible to gather your whole self back completely. *Don't even try.*

Take one final gasp for air and one last grip of all that you think you are. Then, in an instant, release the world you've been clenching with your jaw. Melt into the edges, and disappear into the murky swamp waters.

Feel the weight of a thousand love letters unwritten crush you under the words left unsaid while what's left of you is ripped to shreds. Be swallowed whole. Become numb from the inside out.

From the dark cave that is your grave, a ray of light will burst from the void, expand across the horizon and ride on the wings of the breeze, landing as a soft tickle on your arm.

And you will feel.

It's in this moment, you'll remember what it is to be alive. That death is just the beginning. That light will pull your hollow bones back together and fill them with courage, the cartilage you'll need to bend without breaking.

Resilience will make a permanent residence in your bones.
You'll unlearn the world from this new body, taste truth in the
wake of death.

Cracked open, your heart will be threaded back together by
a thousand singing birds. Forevermore, a song only you can
hear will play in the chambers of your chest, a melody of sweet
sorrow, wherever you are.

Under the warmth of the sun,
your skin will melt
and shiver in the wind.
you'll feel everything,
all at once.

Your eyes will carry the strength of a thousand soldiers while
your soul drifts, wayfinding upon open waters with palms facing
the sun. One day, when rivers merge with the salty breeze, you'll
recognize your reflection, not as you were before, but as you
were always called to become, *soaked by the sun and shadows.*

Only you know what it took to make it here. To put one foot in
front of the other. To stand in the sun while darkness consumes.
Grief has become you like blue becomes the sky before dawn. It
is your bones and blood, and as you stand in the light, love will
pour down from the crown on your head to the tips of your toes
with each glorious step forward.

It will feel overwhelming to hold the pain and such a tender love
for life, but this is your gift to share. Because you'll know the
truth: after darkness is light.

Until then...

let your heart shatter.

// petrichor

i looked for you again
up another mountain top
all i found was
the dew of grief
scattered across
painted skies,
a slow sunrise and
the smell of dust
after rain.

// velvet sea

like a feather
dancing on the waves of wind
she soars in my heart
with unworldly delicacy.

an all-pervading softness,
she is the sun's glow,
energy moving,
melting everything in her path.

ushered into darkness,
expanding under the wings of death,
her smiling eyes –
liberated by stars.

mmm. yes...

held in a velvet sea,
just as i once was,
and always am,
is where i know her to be.

// last words

you're up there,
i'm way down here
i'll never be good enough
i'm a fucking loser...
a worthless
fucking loser...

hannah alley

...she shrunk
shoulders sunk
snot dripped violently down her nose –

my nose

pain howled in her eyes –
a sonderous gaze.

                                                the sun rose in her throat
                                               and light filled the room
                                                       a beautiful
                                                           gentle
                                                     dying soul
                                          surrendered in the night.

// i.f.m.y.m.

It dances on your heart
in the most p e c u l i a r way.
Some would mark it a classic,
                        beautiful, they say.
And maybe it is beautiful, tragically so,
the way it can slice open your chest,
    press
          d
              o
                  w
                      n,
                            with pure precision,
                            slice open your heart
                            so smoothly,
                            and with one chord
                            it turns into a ballad.
                            Echoes in a hollow chamber.

My grief song is full
with scars of regret...
        like the christmas
        i called her a bitch
        refused to answer her calls
        glared disapprovingly,
        avoided her gaze,
        embarrassed to be with her
                from her,
                part of her,
                my first home –
                she birthed me from her womb
                I was nourished by her breasts....
Still letters unwritten,

caged in along with her demons,
locked away and forgotten.
She b e g g e d and p l e a d e d
for a small place inside my heart.
I shoved her aside, put the world between us...

> *you could have showed a little empathy,*
> *you selfish girl.*

Let's not make this another pathetic sad song.
This is a classic,
she'd say,
like Bruce Springsteen.
    give it an impromptu
    sprint on the sax –

> *o n e   l o n g   r u n*
> *to take your pain away.*

In a melody thick as fog
memories cloud my vision...

> *remember that time in my car*
> *when you told me enough –*
> *quit picking at me, you said.*
> *I swallowed my pride,*
> *hid the words behind a smile,*
> *liking how you stood up for yourself.*
> *I couldn't bring myself to say...*
> *you wore your voice well that day.*

Eventually the quick,
sharp stabs
turn into dull throbs,
like a pluck of a string,
l o n g   b u z z   o f   v i b r a t i o n...
    slow
        l i n g e r i n g,

a memento deep in my gut.
Ribs caged by melancholy riffs
played only in minor keys…
you seem better, they say.
      Fuck you, hums gently
      in the back of my throat.

Time is the great healer, they say
The rhythm still cuts like a knife in my side,
a grenade thrown into the unconscious of my mind.
The pain fades, sure,
but it never leaves, not really.
      Triggers are everywhere,
      just like the sky.

The mask I now wear
presents a palpable pain,
a more appropriate sorrow
I can package for work tomorrow…
      and is the sun still shining –
      maybe even more vibrant than before?

I find her in the clouds –
twirling around on the edge of the shore.
She floats by like soft jazz.
      I'll play that one later,
      when I want to torture myself.

Could I just disappear?
really sink inward,
blur the lines and lose myself
somewhere between your face when i found you
and the stolen memories we'll never got to share.
They would understand, i think,
eventually stop calling
with pity heavy on their tongue.
      was it real?

hannah alley

> *you were real –*
> *and so were the sneers your way,*
> *the ones I try not to replay.*
> *They send me into the dark side of my mind like*
> *a broken record of frantic rage...*

I'm listening for the *g o o d   k e y s*
like the softness of your voice
and the gentle tickle of your fingertips on my arm.
The upward gliss of a trumpet
or the trombone that tokes teasingly.
But *ohh*
those minor keys creep back in
s l i p p i n g   into my melody
and here I am, again,
reaching for the sky...
as i repatch old wounds
with photos of your smile
and search for answers
that have no question.

> *You vanished into thin air like*
> *you were never even here.*

August keeps your smiling song
in the corners of his heart.
Time flies
as I float through the seasons,
coming together,
falling apart,
catching you in the light of his eyes.

this...
my beautiful demise.

I fucking miss you, mom.

sun-soaked shadows

hannah alley

There's a lot going on in my mind, body, and the world right now. I'm finding it difficult at times to anchor into the earth… everyone trying to extract from her, maybe that's why. So, I'm here evaluating my relationships. Feet planted, I am grounding in with her energy. Take. Take. Take. Yes. That's it. We're all taking while she gives us life. What do I do with this energy? When I dig my feet deep into the soil, how do my hands give the love in my soul? How am I a channel for that energy to flow? Where do I direct it with my thoughts, with my emotions, and with my actions? There is not *(or is there?)* any 'new' energy being created, rather, we are all accessing and exchanging energy from and with one another. The earth and the sky – so what is wrong with us? When did we forget this sacred foundational principle of living in reciprocity with the land? Is it too late to remember?

Is this separation from God?

sun-soaked shadows

i stepped into
the river
of grief
currents of love
carried me
to new shores.
drifting,
i'm lost and
remembering.

hannah alley

// our bones remember

The legacy of my bones
hums beneath my skin,
like a war cry.
Ancestors calling me home.

Home to my purpose,
of ritual & rites of passage –
feminine pleasure
& pride.

Harmonizing with the land.
A knowing.
The sacred union
between my heart and my hands.

Hips shaped for dancing,
& birthing babies,
At home in red tents
and sisterhood.

Skin that softens at my lover's touch
like flowers reaching for the sun.
Fingers dug deep in the dirt.
Grass-stained skirts.

Eyes wide closed
in the dark,
the truth illuminated
a legacy woven in my bones.

// dreams

Fearful visions fill my night.
Screams stir my body awake
as I lay there frozen in fright.
I want to scream what's in my head
but I whisper instead,
guzzling the darkness
and hide it within.

I speak the words into the still night,
the nightmare that burns my memory.
I am met only with disbelief –
> *that's what you dream about?*
> *not of sun-kissed skin,*
> *fields of flirting sunflowers,*
> *eyes swooning.*
> *lovemaking under the light of the moon?*

Sometimes, yes.
But not this time.
The night served me death and despair,
a betrayal impossible to rewind.

The mind works overtime
to make up happiness.

don't consume the darkness,
step out from the shadows.
breathe + become light.
o p e n.
accept love,
everything's all right.

hannah alley

I am the darkness
and the light.

Should a life of pain
not find solace
in sweet dreams?
I lay in the dark
mourning the death
of a breathing love
reaching again for things I cannot name.

it was just a dream.
it was all only a dream.

When I first dreampt of my mother after her death, it was dark — unstable, she was frantic, lost, searching and I chasing her through a crowded room, chaotic, and without purpose or people I knew.

"She had to "pass through the portal of death and travel through the underworld of (her) own being — s before going to the father — or the great being of her own soul.

I never really understood the meaning or lesson of that dream, or mystical experience of joining her in the dark side of her being for a (shadows) brief moment. Reading of Mary Magdalen recall Yeshua visiting her in his Ka body prior to his own ascension — first to bring power to the Ka and second to either create a trail of light through death itself for people, like my mom, to follow more easily.

→

...rings the hairs on my arm to
attention and the pit of my stomach
... — the only reference I have
... describing her state is the
...ears she experimented and fell
...prey to the evils of meth.
...thin, ^a sunken version of her own
...[s]ight, dimmed by the paralyzing
...[y]et burning affect of the drugs.
... black dress hung on her bones
...s she turned left, then right
...own hallways and through bodies
...tanding shoulder-to-shoulder.

...when I finally caught up to her
...y hand landed on her right
...houlder and she turned her head
...nd looked right through me.

                    my face
I woke up, already drenched
...th my own tears, my
own grief and anguish.
There was nothing I
could do to help her find

// *immortality*

an elixir of life
the life-giving river
fountain of youth
living waters
the nectar of gods
supernatural red wine
the ever-unfolding flower.

my heart leaps from rest
but it's only a feather
dancing weightless on my chest.

coming back to wholeness
by sinking deeper within,
this flesh free falls into the abyss.
a dark cosmic void
is our pathway home.
Rebirth.
a pleasant surprise not to miss.

// she wolf

ethereal whispers
dance on a glimmering crow
it spreads its wings
to escape this cold hard ground.

a shy bluebird
diligently makes its nest
beneath the arresting shade
of an eternal full moon.

she sings a sweet plea to come home.
reaching for the sky
only to fall into the rising sun,
claiming infinite space to roam.

a secret melody shrieks
from the heart of the stars
just before darkness falls
she clears her throat –

let yourself howl, sister.
throw back your head,
open your throat,
let the pain be heard.

// 3am, again

The temperature dropped again.
I can hear the cool air
creep in through
single-pane glass,
hissing my name
as it creeps across my skin.

I stir –
dig my feet
under the belly
of a snoring dog,
searching for warmth
beneath the weight of silk.

I try to settle in –
but i don't drift back
into the dream of me
caught in a wild snowstorm with Flea
or anywhere i'm happy to be.

the ceiling fan
chases stale air.
An eerie lullaby
roars nearby
like daggers
tiptoe...
tiptoe...
across my mind
when suddenly
you breeze by…
I leap…

hannah alley

        Is this when you died?
        You who wakes me each night?
        Sweet of you to swing by,
        to make sure I'm alright
        after I found you, too,
        frozen in the night.

Are you still cold?
That damn yellow knit throw,
was it enough?
What was i thinking –
you were wild-eyed
with lipstick pale blue
slurring nonsense about playing pool.

        I didn't really want
        you to fuck off.
        How could I have known
        just three hours later
        after we wished our goodnights,
        you'd just vanish from my sight –

        and what a sight you were.

It feels more like a blur.
If I had known that hug would be our last
I'd hold you longer,
really make you know,
really let my love show,
allow our love to grow.

We could brew some tea,

share a midnight toke or
cozy under that yellow throw and
laugh over some dumb inside joke.
I'd let you tickle my arm,
or we could dance through the night.
Let's hop in the car
and drive all night if we have to.
We can't rewind but we can close the distance...
I'll take the service roads this time.

For now, I'm gathering bones
among all the stones thrown,
and hidden truths between us.
As your ashes spread
barriers fall and
the walls of my heart tumble.

When dawn draws near
love lifts the veil,
but still...
still, you're not here.

So, I'll look within,
find you when I drop in.
Because here I am,
3 a.m.,
again,
writing this damn poem.

An account of our encounter
so, ma
same time tomorrow?

hannah alley

how can we *not* believe anything is possible?

we are all birthed from a woman's womb,
our cosmic mother,
and a galaxy of infinite vastness -

to be alive is to believe in magic.

// god, is that you?

// the smell of you

The way it felt to be tickled by her –
fingertips with nails chewed to the skin, barely grazing my skin.
The sweet smell of earth dancing around my nose.

Fresh rosemary from my garden simmers in water on the stove. I add a few drops of myrrh, and inhale deeply. It's the closest I've gotten to conjuring her smell. It's close but not quite right. When I add a pinch of patchouli, I find you – a sweet earthy balsamic spice that warms the darkest corners of my heart. I diffuse through the house and anoint my mind's eye as the morning comes to life outside.

It's a rare occasion, usually when I'm least expecting it, I'll smell her, just for a moment. She never lets me hold on too long. *"I'm free, remember?"* She sighs and loosens her grip, vanishing to dance on the waves of the ocean and soar as the wind through the trees. The branches above me sway her freedom dance and I smile, squinting at the sun peaking through the lanky romance of the eucalyptus tree. The trunk twists from the hips, sending its branches into beautiful formation. A bird has made her nest, and she sings a sweet song as I sit here under the hush of the wind, witnessing the magic of it all.

Thank you tree –
there's something to be said of how you've rooted and stood tall with history etched into your trunk, and here you sway in such sweet synchronicity with the wind, never asking permission to be seen. Existing all the same.

I think myrrh is the lost scent of my soul.
Patchouli is yours.

friday 7.10

The way it felt to be tickled by her — her fingertips w/ nails chewed to the skin — barely grazing my skin. her sweet smell of earth danced around us.

Rosemary water, a few drops of myrrh, and ~~the~~ half drop of pachouli — it the closest I've gotten to conjuring her smell. otherwise, on the rare occassion, and usually when I'm least expecting it, I'll smell her in a moment — though she never lets me hold on too long — "I'm free, remember" — ~~last night~~ and I let her go or she vanishes to dance in the waves of the ocean or ~~party~~ soar with the wind through the ~~trees~~. The branches above me sway, echoing that I live a I can't help but look up and smile, squinting at the sun peaking through the ~~totally~~ lanky branches of this free-formed Eucalyptus tree, whose trunk twists at the hips, bending its limbs into beautiful formation. A birds made her nest and sings a sweet song to her babes and I sit here, under the hush of the wind witnessing the magic of it all. Thank you tree —

there's something to be said about how a tree, rooted and standing tall w/ history etched into its trunk sways in such sweet synchronicity w/ the wind, and never asks ~~for perm~~ permission, or begs to be seen — ~~she just is~~ she exists ~~without~~...

Take a deep breath.
You're safe.

Close your eyes, and
let these words imprint on your heart.

You have a voice
to be heard.

You have a gift
to be shared.

You have a touch
to be felt.

You have a message
to be spread.

You are worthy of being seen.

Step into the light,
and let the sun shine down.

// You are what the world needs

hannah alley

How dare the world continue to spin
as time stands still in the wake of losing you.

the roar
of a woman
in metamorphosis.

the shedding
of skin
through sacred portals.

a sweet dance
with death
to birth
new life.

the rebirth
of self.

// metamorphosis

hannah alley

Wombyn.
The womb keepers –
the great dreamers,
grand creators,
life-givers
weaving the world
with their beating hearts.

Always birthing,
curating consciousness,
expressing,
nurturing

A budding seed,
rooted in the womb of our mother.
We all blossom
from soil of infinite possibility

Woman.
Women.
Women.
    the womb of a woman.
Wombyn.

Suppressing the womb
is to rid the world of magic,
wildflowers
& weeds.

Can you imagine?
What a bummer life would be.

// wombyn

The morning calm
is a slow dance with the sea.
Sitting here, choosing who I'll be...
this is my great unbecoming.

The hum and sighs
awaken with the sun,
and I am a loving witness,
the sea and I are one.

I find my breath
as birds gather seeds from the ground.
The wind greets us,
gratitude is all around.

The ocean invites inner peace
with loving conviction.
Waves pull me deeper
into the depths of the unknown.

Surrender to her and she'll carry you,
wash you onto new shores.

There are always new shores.

And she sings,

"La playa
las risas
todo es magia
si tu crees.
Es un buen día."

// immersed

hannah alley

the portal of infinite possibilities

a gateway to every you

at every time –

the cosmic doorway home.

when wombyn
step into their power
as the creatrix
anything is possible.

// g is for grief

The world is magic,
I hope you can see
there's beauty around each corner.
In you,
it's also in me.

But in life, things happen -
I'm sure by now you know,
that leaves us swirling,
lost, believing magic
comes with a cost.

Grief is the word we give to love
when it's stuck in your throat,
and heavy on the chest.
It rings dull in your ears,
rips your gut,
and will go on for years.

And even still,
it's warm on your skin,
like the sun in spring.
Gentle as the breeze
like a playful tease,
there are no rules in grief,
              not really.

at the end of the day,
if we still find laughter
during long winter days
that's when we know
we'll all be okay.

hannah alley

grief doesn't shrink
over   time
i'm just able to
carry   the   weight
now without breaking.

// *good time girl*

deep connections
with myself,
my sisters,
gaia,
the universe.

stretching with the rising sun
& slow mornings
that slip into soft sunsets.

fresh herbs
for afternoon tea.

sensual poetry
while myrrh incense burns.

laughter and foreplay,
getting lost in the woods.

slow dancing under the stars.

expanding on the release...

a sovereign being
as free as the sun
is my kind of fun.

hannah alley

// coconino

and this is my life now
dancing through ferns,
escaping poison oak.
my cheek to the wind
hair kissed by the sun
and as night falls,
i'll be singing
under a canopy of stars.

savoring stillness
this is pure bliss.

// middle of nowhere

cool crisp air
wind-tossed hair.
sunsets melting
your hand to share.

as above
so below the mountains
warm smiles
spirits bouncing.

in the forest
my heart is found.
lost in big bear
out in the middle of nowhere.

hannah alley

// *the sweetness of time*

slow down
take   your   time
honor
          the   sweet
                    sweet   divine.

// wet soil & serpentine

there is no pot that sits
at the end of a rainbow
only damp soil
where the serpentine lives –

        but look closely...

and discover kisses s o   s l o w
and *so sweet.*
nirvana lives
on the edge of the abyss –
and should you fall
    – I hope you do –
you'll find repeated bliss

and repeated bliss

and repeated bliss

golden rivers *flow like wine*
and sunshine slips
up and down your spine.

ecstasy rests with those lips
draped
      wrapped
cocooned
in the sky's embrace.
we swim as one.

hannah alley

so uncurl your toes –
        you're safe
unfold from the hips –
        you're safe
and bloom from within.
        welcome home.

so, let go..
allow life to flow
and unfold from your chest.
free fall into paradise.
beneath a sea so divine
is the seat of your soul.

letting go is *gold* / fucking sublime.

// undone with the one

my dear, your lips
spread into the smile
of a rising sun,
in your eyes
i come undone.
in the sweet surrender
of dawn,
my dear,
i'm holding you here.

// *w.i.p.*

her love is free flowing,
and she's rooted in her worth.

boundaries are set
with reverence.

"there's enough sunshine for us all to bathe under," she says.

she rises before dawn
to root her feet in the soil.
food grown by her hands,
she tends to her garden
like she mends a tender heart -
daily, with compassion.

she allows nature to nurture,
ancestors to guide,
ideas to breathe,
with the courage to birth them.

humor is her medicine
because she knows
there's always room for play.
her home, a creative expression…
she's a masterpiece,
and a work in progress.

// mystic in the mirror

when you discover
the mystic rhythm of your body,
you find the magic
in all things.

when you discover
the magic in all things,
you see the mystic
in the mirror.

hannah alley

// pink bottom girls

"there's enough sunshine
for us all," she said.

and so
we all bathed
together
under the
warm waves
until our skin
turned pink.

sun-soaked shadows

// supai, 2020

Heavy rain turned turquoise pools brown and mucky just before we hiked down into the canyon. Each night I slipped into sleep with the steady sound of currents flowing, and woke to a new shade of blue. I was amazed by water's commitment to healing, releasing what holds it back from flowing freely, returning to its purest form. A continuous flow of love. The process of becoming.

Could I be like that water?

What can I learn from nature's rhythm and flow, especially now when people are feeling a deep sense of loss – jobs, routines, loved ones. How can we surrender to the emotional pace of loss, find wisdom in it, and transmute it to something beautiful? Everything we've gripped so tightly to as our compass and sense of reality is lifting – being swept away with the strength of our collective current, with the desire to return to our purest form. The dark waters are being called home for a reckoning with the sea. The great return to ourselves, to our essential nature.

Do you, too, seek the stillness to hear the currents deep within you? Step into the waters of your own inner river, and may we all flow like water and wash away the muck.

And so it is.

wisdom is expansion. And expansion happens on the exhale - the release. My moms death also symbolized the death of my ego which kept me small, vibrating low in my lower chakras — and w/ that clearing, grew a stronger knowing of my personal power and inner wisdom to bring my gifts into the world.

truth & love
are permeate

The red heart of ma'at is my
love — a knowing. place it in my
ma'at and let my voice be an
expression of my heart.

— The truth of Ma'at —

when you feel in indecision —
it's not a matter of the mind,
it's of the heart. A truth
weaver — just measure it
all against the feather

the feather   what is my truth?
as small in my   — from here I'll know
and then shifted   where to walk —
to a large
black feather
upright next to me that fell in my arms for me
                    to cradle like a baby,
                    & then back home
                    to my ∞

this idea of a womb being the galaxy's
reflection — we all come from galactic
source, emerging from the womb & b[lank]
taking earth form — taking our first breath
we're all polluting our bodies —
a temple, activation space, so our soul
be hidden — just as we emerge for our
1st breath to be polluted w/ sour air,
artificial light, & deafening sounds.

hannah alley

// truth is weightless

trust
the
sweet
breeze
of
truth

that dances in your heart.

sun-soaked shadows

// more

as we whispered
our plans to the horizon
waves rolled in
like laughter onto shore.
we stood there holding hands,
licking salt from our lips,
no longer craving more.

hannah alley

// sweet child of mine

he's the fertilizer of my life right now,
allowing me to sprout roots and grow in places
i had never known.

// kids can't be caged

don't cage me in,
she shouts in her head
smiling through her teeth
words left unsaid.

she does as she's told,
a good little girl,
easy to mold
it seems to those in charge.

yet nobody knows
the world in her mind
dreams vast & wide
no structure for her to hide.

exposed –
heart on her sleeve
living among those
who can't be tamed.

building wings in the night
dreaming her escape
of all she's known herself to be
to a day her mind will finally fly free.

but today,
she's in a single file line
playing just fine.

hannah alley

playful
full of adventure
meaningful
intentional
passionate

home in my own skin
comfortable wherever i am

connected
creative
fulfilled
mystical
sensual
expansive

i am not ambivalent in my life.

I am not Ambivalent in my life

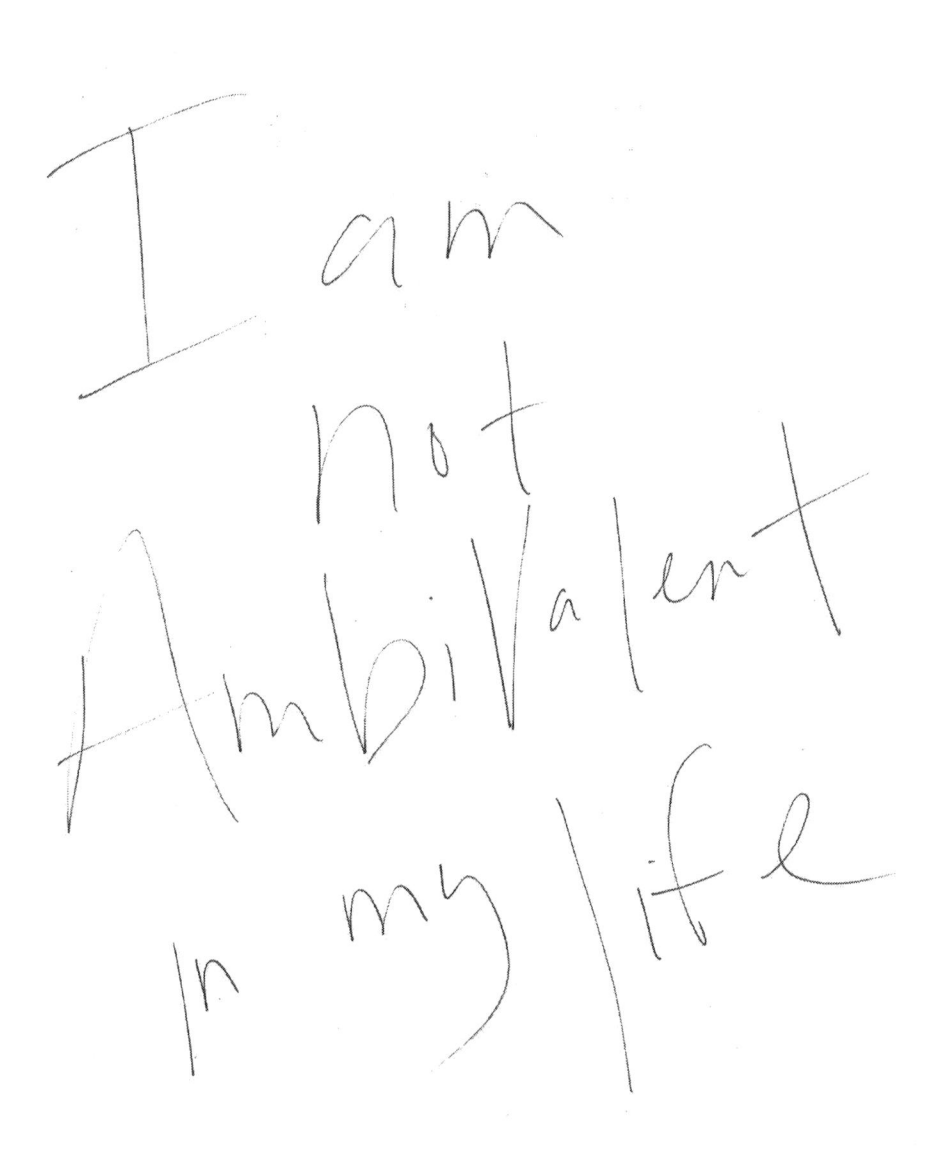

// benevolent

I am not ambivalent.

I do not want a life of ambivalence.

I am not ambivalent in my life.

I want a life of benevolence.

I am benevolent in my life.

I am benevolent.

// connected to the flow

i'm grateful
for the wind that blows,
rivers that flow
a sun to rise
and colors
that flirt in the sky.

grateful for the heat,
the breeze,
and sand
beneath my feet.

for the desert,
love,
a sense
of where i belong
and, lastly,
for Jess' naan.

hannah alley

// *mirrors*

we are
as vast as the sky,
sacred as the land
a reflection -
so divine.

// *wakan*

the world remains in slumber
to the universal wonder
of the wind –
      it plays keys
      unlocking the code –
w e   a l l   w i n
when we listen
to the wisdom
beating from our heart –
it mirrors what's etched
in the grooves of bark,
adorned by moss –
      a mark
it is sacred to be human,
to feel the sun on our skin
& pass stories of our ancestors
on to our kin.

in the company of rocks
we witness the free form of hawks –
      free as the sky,
the token prize to be alive.

keepers of this earth
here to tend to the land
sink hands in soil
& feel the roots of our soul.

the knowers of trees,
we speak the language of bees,
when we're not too distracted
by destruction and disease.

hannah alley

protect Oak Flat,
the birds,
breeze,
the air we breathe.

progress means
to plant more seeds;
growth is to grow back
      reconnect.

the sun is setting on greed,
as we rise in the spiral
glowing with the universal knowing
all are sacred,
wakan,
we are one.

connected by this thread –
to care means
neither the air,
nor the land,
are for sale.

sun-soaked shadows

We cannot weave together
what believes it is seperate
only what yearns to be one

‖ true unity

hannah alley

// what if we gave the land back?

the land belongs to no human.
this is why
we can't feel the thread
of connection
because we believe
the soul of land
can be owned,
claimed,
loaned.

it's a living,
breathing,
sacred being
to be loved
and acknowledged.
we are humble visitors,
children of the sky and soil,
thread together in sacred ritual.

belonging means connected,
respect so we aren't longing
for what was.
we can't possess
what can't fit in our grave.

we cannot weave together
what believes it is separate...
only what yearns to be one.

who could we be
if we gave the land back
to the great mystery?

// root wisdom

we are all fractals of light
reflecting the same thing
through different windows.
a beautiful kaleidoscope
of perspective and experience.
a complex web of vivid expression.

i will not exploit this
in the name of separation
but honor it,
call in remembrance,
oneness
and live like a great oak,
is to live by the sacred knowings,
and be witness to root wisdom.

hannah alley

// medicine prayers

i hope you are swept up
in love today,
held so tenderly
your skin melts.
i hope your heart sings
your hips into swing
and you somersault
under the sun -
free as the wind.

another time,
another place
somewhere far far away
from this damn rat race
we're all swept up
riding waves of ecstacy.
waking with a cool breeze
under a hot sun
we remember our mission
and come together.

let this be our
p r e m o n i t i o n.

sun-soaked shadows

what if death

hannah alley

is the beginning?

// *dying to live*

When we grip so tightly to life, we forget to breathe and spend our days trying to catch our breath. Is this why generations continue to choke on the air? We're inhaling pollution, toxic thoughts and despair when we could trust the free-fall of our exhale. The sweet release is a full embrace of newfound space.

Our breath is always leading us to new terrain, whispering "it's safe to let go."

The death of an inhale is the spark of life. Birth repeats, again and again, in the natural cycle of breath. Our mystic path of limitless unfolding, and *to allow death is to fully live. We're all dying to live.* Yet, we're afraid of the spaciousness death offers us.

That's it.

Death is contaminated by fear.

Damn you, fear, always spoiling our fun.
Keeping us hostage on the edge of depth,
only half-living in a shallow breath.

Why do we run from this inevitable fate rather than lean in with reverent curiosity? Could that shift us from fear to freedom? From a culture afraid of death to a world free to live? How can death expand our sense of love and community? What happens when we unfold our arms to death as a catalyst for life, ushering us into new beginnings?

What ideals, beliefs, behaviors can we collectively shed to reimagine a new earth?

hannah alley

death brings purification,
which allows space
for us to integrate,
rebirth,
and become
again, and again.

sun-soaked shadows

// happy is in the details

We all have our own idea of what happiness is,
but then it shows up in the smallest and most insignificant
of ways, and it throws us off because isn't happiness this big
tangible thing that you can wrap your arms around, drive around
with, hold in your hands, and roll around in?

I don't know what I'm saying, and maybe I don't know much.
But, I feel with all my being – the look on my little man's face
as we scooted ourselves through the streets of San Francisco,
with the cool breeze expanding my lungs, was what I can only
describe as pure, unadulterated happiness.

I think I'm happy in the details,
and that's enough.

hannah alley

our deepest wound
　　　is our greatest gift

we try and control the flow of water
as if we don't know we're the
whole damn river.

we try & control the flow of water
as if we aren't the whole damn river.

hannah alley

we try and control
   the flow of water
     as if we aren't
the whole damn river.

We are the whole damn river.

sun-soaked shadows

// a conversation with my shadow

hannah alley

I can't even look at you.

> Why, what do you see?

Darkness. Trash. A girl unworthy of anything good in this world. A complete disappointment. Any love that may slip into your grip will eventually run off, leaving you alone.

> All light comes from darkness.
> A galaxy of stories radiate from these eyes – lean in,
> do you see?

I see a life I want to replace.
Memories to lock in the back closet of my mind

> Our deepest wounds are the source of our greatest gifts.
> I'll always be this story you're trying to outrun
> if you can't accept me.

I can't even look at you.

> Try? Look at me like you would your son.
> Open your heart and allow me to be part of
> your journey now.

I'm afraid.

> Of what?

What if there's only darkness?

> What if you're the light?

// winds of change

we are not static beings,
rigid in our decisions
but complex, vivid beings
with the innate right to pivot at any point.

hold the vision, write the plan…
but do not hold it so tightly
that you ignore the whispers
longing to ride the winds of change.

// eclipse

wrapped around my mind
like the moon's soft glow
stretching across
the river of time
the shadows reveal
bodies in divine flow

your smile inches across my skin –
a cool breeze gliding curiously
beneath a blanket of trees
…where lush forest
melts into wetlands
and flowers blush
with each touch.
we explore below
the canyon's cliff
drenched in golden light
together,
we dance to an endless riff
synchronizing with the slow drift of stars

worlds apart
common, baby
eclipse my heart.

// queen of swords

seeker with
a beautiful mind
a woman who knows
how to take her time.
purveyor of truth –
she's straight to the point.
the loneliness in her heart
is wisdom
carried from the start.
a sharp intellect
never at rest
is a weapon she keeps
close to her chest.
a queen on her throne
with a perspective all her own.

hannah alley

her laughter
rings in my bones
waves of smiles
cross my face
aged by love
deepend with desire.

// a winding road is more fun to travel

For the first time, I believe my path is unfolding in perfect synchronicity, yet I find myself fighting it with a self-sabotaging vengeance. Lulled by the sensual nature of our existence, the thread which connects us pulls me closer to unity, melting into the milky waves of oneness, where my essence swims. It's here I discover the unique divinity of me. And, there's an all-consuming desire to run in the name of separation, hide from the whispers in the trees, close my eyes to the magic of the seemingly unseen, and follow the well-paved path. That sweet hum reverberates in the soft tissue of my spine, right on the edge of escape, inviting me to step outside into the sun.

warm waves pulse within
and I suddenly feel fine –
this is sweeter than any sip of wine.
nature is always here to remind
when we're so quick to forget.
it's here I come alive,
and remember the divine.

hannah alley

nature in rhythm
shows us
how to let go,
allows our
minds to be in flow,
so we can be
as free as the wind.

// try everything once, twice if you like it

as i close my eyes
these pools of blue
are wrapped
in an ocean of forest green
and where shadows dance
across canyon cliffs
is where i dream of us.

the sun, my fire
playfully tamed
by your breeze
the leaves
sway in celebration
that two souls would
find each other
again and again.
again.
again.
let's do it again.

hannah alley

there's a glistening
dancing along the shoreline,
the moon glows above
and the air is thick with salt
the rocks are damp
with moss &...

// *damp thoughts*

// scorpio moon

quench my thirst
under this hot
hot desert sun –
it's the curse
of the scorpion gulch

grab the cup,
fuck…
i'll drink the moon
first
swallow her glow
and cool this hollow womb
with an overflow of venom
from a bottomless well

how far is the ocean?
let's go tonight,
chase a swelled sunrise
just one more sip
      reaching
      releasing
      sweet surrender
drown in desert waves.

// soul shine

her soul shined through pained eyes
as her heart bled for younger days,
like a star she blazed
so bright until she burned
right through her innocence.

Jethro Tull to Springsteen
she danced with her eyes wide shut,
hands out wide to every melody.
never turned her back on a sunset
or a stranger,
she was the kindest woman i ever met.
now she sleeps among the stars.

be strange

hannah alley

not strangers

want to know the secret to a life worthy of living?

it's simple, she said.

never turn your back on a sunset or a stranger.

hannah alley

// red rocks

as the great blue sky
dances in our eyes
dusk falls to night
and souls collide
just right.

// disaster on the inside

you say you're mine
i hear the words
but,
       how high will you climb?
the road to me
is paved with misery
the hoops, the mountains,
the tricks up my sleeve…
       you'll never measure up,
i'll make sure you feel every bump.

the diamond you're trying to find,
       buried deep on the inside
is all an illusion of the mind –
my sweet little lie.

the cave you mine
is full with coal
and, inevitably,
destruction will come knocking on your door.

so, when i'm standing there,
begging you to come in –
       don't answer.

       save yourself from this disaster.

hannah alley

// taking radical responsibility for my own healing

my mind swirls
in your wavering plans.
my heart feels unsafe
in your trembling hands.

but how could you know
the power of a tender touch
when you've only ever seen
women turn to stone under the hot sun.

i'll take my heart back for a while,
and learn to trust my own smile.

// *all the ways to love*

how are you loving
your bones
and your blood?
your skin
and your feet?
can you love any stranger you meet?
do you love the body you're in?

show me by the way
you love the soil
and the trees –
how you love
even through dis-ease.

show me how you love another
by the way you honor
the womb of your mother.

do you love the land?
show me
by the way you drink water
and treat each creature
as a sacred son
and sacred daughter.

show me how you love life
by how you release your grip
and hold reverence for death.
do you remember
not to hold your breath?

hannah alley

how do you love your kin?
show me by the way
you care for each word you say,
in the gestures you display.

show me how you love
like a great force that brings truth -
a pure ray from the sun
that shines as divine proof.

show me
all the ways you love.

// don't pick the weeds

she danced wildly among the wildflowers,
        swung from the branches of her dreams.

her mind a field of blooming petals,
it never occurred to her
to weed her ambition
in favor of becoming a wallflower.

have you ever
stumbled upon a field of dandelions
and thought,
they should really spray for weeds.

of course not
       in the wild
     there are no words for beauty
   beauty simply *is*
when you're wise enough to feel it
in your own wild heart.

// let me show you

every inch of you,
the depths of your being,
deserves to be seen
fully known & completely
for the majestic star
and mystery you are.
let me love you.
open your heart to this river
of love -
i want to pour into you,
you worthy,
cosmic masterpiece of
sovereign creation.
let me find myself
lost in the gaze
of your galactic globe
      of cosmic divinity.
i will touch you
in reverence of the sun
and witness the edges melt
from the warmth
of your core.
seeing you soften
is like being wrapped
in the night sky.
i dive into your silky sea
in search of pearls –
every star aligns
in perfect serendipity
until flowers drip
sweet nectar
my soul longs to taste.

sun-soaked shadows

the greatest tragedy
is to keep a flower from budding.

hannah alley

show me how you love
like a great force
bringing truth.

a pure ray of the sun
that shines as divine proof.

// love right under your nose

she's here,
there,
everywhere.
she wraps me a blanket
weaved by a forest of oaks.
she kisses me
with the warmth of the sun.
i feel her…
like the breeze on my skin
her love is like diving
into a sea as soft as silk.

her laughter is children playing
and i see her
in the shimmy of leaves.

oh, sweet girl, she's there.
just close your eyes and listen.
do you feel her smiling?
now, look in the mirror.
she's right here.

hannah alley

// sun spirit

    she shines through the cracks of ordinary moments
                      sacred rays on my back,

        i feel her r i s i n g
        up each vertebrae

      reaching for a sweet kiss on the crown of my head.

sun-soaked shadows

like the river
meets the sea
you flow into me,
like a drop
in the ocean
you're part of me.

the whole ocean
in a drop
is your memory,
soaked in devotion.

// drops of devotion

// *fleshly desire*

what do i want?

an unconditional love,
as free as the world,
without rigid expectations for who i should be
i am allowed to change my mind, anytime.

give me strong hands with a firm touch
      so i know i can soften my voice,
lean onto you
      & into my heart.

a man unafraid to dive in,
      willing to get messy on the inside,
brave enough to stand in the light.

i want a love that wanders,
collects beauty from all the cobwebbed corners of yesterday –
      to share lessons of better days.

i want a wild love
    primal
        that celebrates the carnal,
uplifts sensual pleasures
      free of inhibition.

i want a love that plants seeds in the mystic
to grow like wildflowers in the wind.
rooted,
and swaying
hand-in-hand.

sun-soaked shadows

can we nurture the sweet unfold,
and celebrate the long slow
dance of becoming?

|| slow dance w/ death

// let's free fall for a while

don't fold yourself in
when the walls of the cave fall in.
life's contractions are a path that keeps winding.
still up the mountain i go
to guzzle the breeze
and swing from tree to tree.

jumping into the mystery of it all
is where i find you…
carried by the universe
it might be scary at first
but you'll be carried by the universe.

// everywhere, and in my heart

hey,
it's been a while,
like forever and a day,
but in my heart you're with me
every step of the way.

you're with the birds –
high in the sky, *flying free*
reminding me it's ok
to just be.

dontcha know
you're the grooviest tune
i feel you flow
sometimes all afternoon.

you're the whistle of a wren
singing high on the breeze
like a curve in the wind –
you go just as you please.

it takes just one song,
played on soft summer leaves,
to remind me
i'm right where i belong.

you're the night sky –
glistening with stars that shine
like the light in your eyes,
reminding me love can fly.
if ever that glow grows dim,
you're there to show me.

hannah alley

love can always be found
if i just look within.

your love has been with me
since the day i was born,
it won't ever leave me,
it only transforms.

so, i let you flow always
and watch you take form…
you're everywhere.
everywhere and in my heart.

sun-soaked shadows

the difference between a thought

                                        & knowing

                                                                                           is how it feels...

hannah alley

...maybe we're all walking around

        spilling our grief on the floors

                for each other to slip over.

sun-soaked shadows

Strange Love

It's been 48 days since I last saw your face, I think, as I stare ahead, memorizing the lines around his mouth. He's speaking, but I'm just looking at his face. I wonder if my eyes are glazed over, and if he can tell I'm in reflective observation. I've changed. He and I both know it, yet when I look into the deep well of his eyes, I don't detect any signs of tragedy. It's as if that big, bad thing never happened.

We're at the neighborhood bar around the corner from the house we share, and I'm half here. I know I'm responding, but most of me is reaching inside his heart to feel his truth. Who is this man sitting across from me? What is he thinking when he smiles? What's the texture of his soul? This is all that has mattered to me since we planted her ashes in the soil.

These are the only topics that interest me these days, the ones that dive into the deep well of despair to recover the soul-shattering secrets of the universe, and rejoice in the mystical moments that leave us in awe. I know I'm in the deep end. I can't bring myself to the shallows – death has made this all too real. My heart sits on the outside of my chest and I'm raw. Tender. If you could see me on the inside, I'm broken-hearted on the bathroom floor, dry-heaving.

Does he even realize I'm not interested? Can he even see me? How is everyone around us carrying on with their lives like I'm not carrying this big thing? It feels so visible, like a ball of fire burning in my chest as strangers smile and our eyes glide past one another. Her body could be lying in front of me, and we'd all be laughing, pretending not to see.

Resentment gets the better of my brows, and I catch the softness of his gaze. His hand reaches across the table and slips over mine. We sit in silence and he smiles into the darkness.

A small light flickers.

I wonder how many of these strangers sit here with grief hanging in the backs of their throats like skeletons in a closet. I wish I knew so I could see myself in their eyes. Do I look as hallow as I feel? I'm learning how to hold all this pain without suffocating from the weight of it all. Maybe I'm constantly seeking the look of sorrow, but it looks a lot like drinks with friends, and I guess I'm finding it in the eyes of strangers. *And lovers.*

He sits across from me, smiling, while the world around us continues on. I quietly count all the ways my mom loved him. How she's found such pride in the life we are building here... she called him "my guy." Her eyes were bright knowing her daughter was loved so well. I can't allow that to be in vain. *Besides, how could I love anyone who didn't know you?*

Maybe we're all walking around spilling our grief on the floors for each other to slip over. It feels surreal, living with this hole in my chest while the faces around me smile for the weekend. And maybe it's okay for me to smile, too.

sun-soaked shadows

When your Bones *just* Know

hannah alley

"I'm going to marry him…" I whispered to the still night. The air was warm with the promise of rain, yet there was none in sight. It was the first dewy night since those days of non-stop rain, and the smell of creosote was dancing in my nose. A pastel-painted sunset was drenched across the skyline, and I was looking out at the horizon seeing my future more clearly than I had in 25 years. He was who I was going to marry. My bones knew it.

I held this knowing softly to my chest as it imprinted throughout my body with a resounding *yes*. I think what is true first takes shape in the body. What you do with that sensation is a choice.

When something is true, there's a melting quality to my breath. My skin and bones are overcome by a silky waterfall I feel safe enough to fall into. It may start in my forehead, a softening of my eyebrows, like my mind has just released its grip of something it couldn't understand and as soon as it's free, the truth cascades down my body. Warm waves wash over my bones, flow around the soft tissue in the darkest corners of my body, melting tension, opening doors that have been locked, and awakening parts of myself that were dormant.

Within all this, something rises like a feather, dancing in my heart and on the surface of my skin, a soft tickle.

Truth is weightless.

// *February*

the day you took your last breath
the clouds parted
and tears poured
from the sky for three days.

for weeks people talked about
the crazy weather we had.

even in death,
i love that you give
them something to talk about.

hannah alley

// let's live, kid

i often think,
will you remember this day?

rain poured down from skies so gray
and i don't think i recall
anything i did until
her celebration that may.

you ask why mommy's sad,
and i try to shake it away
"are you sad your mom's dead"
tears pool in my eyes
and you understand what's been said,
"i wish no one ever died."

and there i think –
and finally find the words to say,
oh, but we do.
death is the only certainty we have.
so this…
this is why we live.

// *spirit embodied*

i've really missed this, she said,
blushing like a pink sunset
through draped eucalyptus.

without a moment of thought
i let her take form
guiding my body into movement.
my feet became drums to the earth,
and we danced until the sun melted into night.

hannah alley

// lonely

loneliness is the shadow
of missing individuality
it disappears
when we find the bridge
that links us together –
just as there's danger
of being swallowed by the crowd.

sun-soaked shadows

I'm here so fully right now. The pines quiver in the wind and light dances across the land with the rising sun as crystal blue glows from my throat. There's something to be said as purifying rays of medicine flow freely. I breathe them down to my centers of matter but the bridge is still under repair. I'm meant to be here, in this space, listening for now. No specific messages have risen to the tip of my tongue or are ready to glide across my head or the paper beneath my hand. I pause.

Birds are chirping and Bogey is pacing on alert – I can feel his anxiety heavy on my chest. He's beautiful all the same. Hand to heart, I take a deep breath.

On the exhale, he sits.

Together, we relish in the stillness of this sun-soaked morning.

hannah alley

// quantum birth

quantum is a hidden ocean
the birthplace of everything
that exists inside,
and outside our minds.

the mother –
spring of all creation.
the source
from which love flows
and flows
to the surface.

sun-soaked shadows

It takes tremendous energy
to rise above your own conditioning,
but the power of inertia is strong.

    I see you.

    I feel you.

    I am you.

hannah alley

music
is both
a medicine and
a drug

it can
heal
and
swallow
you whole.

sun-soaked shadows

I want to see more of the world, she said.

And you should –

just be sure to also show the world more of you.

hannah alley

// gratitude practice

i don't mind
being the first to wake
these quiet moments
i'm more than happy to take.

as the sun slips through the cracks in the curtain
i feel the warmth spread across my bed,
it mirrors the gentle upward curve of my lips
as i witness the slow rise of joy in my heart.

this.
this right here.
is it.

the gateway to a magical realm
a doorway within
the passageway to wisdom
source of enlightenment
infinite power
pure love
the portal to connection
a cosmic cradle of illuminating darkness
a throne of potential
infinite possibility
limitless
a black hole of nothingness, from which all is born
an awakening
the window to all things
the incubator for life
the birthplace of all creation
our first home.

// the womb

hannah alley

// jumping into the void

you learn how to live
when you finally learn
to trust yourself.

the universe is so vast
and i know i am so small,
but size is relative
and tomorrow feels big
so i'll rise to the occasion.

sun-soaked shadows

    the sea is wide
so, there's plenty of time
  to find my stride.

hannah alley

i'm sitting here in the town that made me
a distant memory from where i am now
no longer aching with nostalgia
or longing for a happier tomorrow
those slow,
simple
waves of energy that move mountains
are centuries apart.

// the town that made me

// *a lifetime of guilt*

the last time I held you, I didn't want to let go.
the ambulance was coming and I knew this was it,
our final goodbye, hours too late for saving.
you are gone, with God now.

I crawled into your bed,
wrapped myself around you.
your skin cold,
but still yours.
sun-kissed with freckles,
still vibrant considering the life you've lived.
I rested my tear-stained face on your hardening body
tracing the scar of your generation
I always loved that scar.

like memorizing test answers,
I was mesmerized by your face.
I didn't want to remember you this way,
but I let it burn into my memory
knowing I'd have to fight to see your smile,
hear your laughter,
for all my tomorrows.

no one prepares you for what it's like
to stare death in the face:
the first i time was in high school
drunk driving on the backroads
maybe he fell asleep,
no attempt to miss the tree.
am i allowed to touch the dead?
I kissed my hand
and placed it on his cheek.

startled by the cold, i didn't pull away.
mesmerized by his physical body –
this skin his soul chose was perfect
and I knew there would never be one like it.

"I love you, mom."
"I'm sorry."

I floated out of your room
numb
as they prepared your body.
I was sick at the thought
of them touching you
knowing you would hate this,
being touched by men
in the safety of your bed.

another thing I can choke on later.

they carried you,
pausing for our final goodbye.
what do you say
to a zipped up black body bag
holding your mother's dead body,
with strangers surrounding you?

I flung myself over you,
tearful mumbles muffled
by this cheap plastic between us
snot dripping.

then they took you.

you became property.
there has to be another way

other than sending your body back to jail,
a cold cell as you await your sentence.
but no one prepares you for this moment.
there's no handout, *what to do if your mom overdoses in your home...*

why is it illegal to bury your loved ones in your backyard?

your oldest son wanted to break you out of jail,
tried to convince us it's what you'd want.
maybe you would. a jailbreak.

from that moment on, I hated myself for spending 28 years of my life pushing you away, avoiding your calls, slipping out of your hugs, and guarding my heart from your tender touch.

hannah alley

back to the womb
a thousand lifetimes healed
our last words wrapped in that hug
still, i let go too soon.

// why do bad things happen to good people?

was it drugs?
the doctors that overprescribe?
big pharma and all of their disgusting lies?
was it the politicians for not giving a fuck,
blinded by greed,
disguised by small humanitarian deeds?
was it growing up with an alcoholic mother?
the maternal trauma passed down daughter to daughter?
was it inherited from the womb?
because of the unfortunate blessing
of being born a girl?
is it because you almost died as a child?
because you were the favorite?
raped and molested?
was it because you are an Aquarius,
the rebels of the zodiac?
what a bizarre turn of events.
was it postpartum depression?
was it leaving your kids?
was it not coming back?
was it guilt? shame?
did you think we wouldn't forgive you?
was it because if your slum-lord, karen?
was it choosing the wrong men,
    abusive men who stole from your giving heart?

was it all in God's plan?
fate?
was it past life karma?
because of my Saturn return?

was it because of the way society treats drug users?

because you wore the scars of your past?

was it because you were labeled "unemployable"?
was it hiring you on the spot?
or firing you when your background check came back?
was it because of the letter you wrote,
begging them to reconsider?

was it the heartbreak of unrealized dreams?
did your disappointment overpower your sense of hope?
was it depression?
because of desperation?
was it your criminal record?
because you were homeless?
was it all the time you spent in jail?
was it the meth that caused you to lose all your teeth?

is it because of pollution?
hormone-injected meat?
too much soy?

is it because we live on stolen land?
because Grandma Tillie was adopted?
is it because our ancestors were murdered?
was it because the land is poisoned?
because of climate change?
is it our disconnection from nature?
the lost indigenous wisdom of your ancestors?

was it because i was a bad kid?
did i not breastfeed well enough?
was i not worth sticking around?
was it because i didn't hug you more,
love you more?

i guess i'll never know.

sun-soaked shadows

how do you stop a river
flowing deep
washing away the debris
unseen
beneath the surface
you'll keep
nothing left,
you are wiped clean.

An evening under the stars
with my heart pressed against her, aching
the steady hum   like the teachings of Ast
vibrating beneath me.   I've become
                        hidden in
I listen to the   hardened behind
wisdom of her body   secret walls
the truth of her fertility.

what is my connection
to this earth?

who are my ancestors?
what have I come here
       to do?

Ast, sing to me in my
   dreams. let my soul remember
on this new moon and
   let this seed I'm planted
sprout

// allow me to rise

Who am I?
Who am I?

 I repeat over and over as my eyes lie closed. I'm in the arena with the horses and I can feel their presence, yet I can't feel my own. I begin to breathe the words through me, witnessing the release in my muscles, my bones. The wind whips through.
 I am the wind.
 The horses grow louder, then stop as soon as I bring my attention to them. We are attuned. Am I holding my breath? Release. Slip deeper. "Who am I?" melts away and I am... floating. I feel Ruby over me, looking down and I am easily pulled out of the current. Ruby nudges my left knee with her snout.

 I'm so easily pulled out, I think. She nudges me again. This time with more force before walking past. Confirmation. I feel her presence to my left and yearn for her return. I'm alone. Of course I am. Another story that keeps me trapped in loneliness. Back to my breath. Flies surround me and the buzzing etches across my skull.

Who am I?

 I am enough. *Yes.* Breathe into that. I expand my breath and make an audible exhale, drawing in air, expanding my breath, grasping to fill the space between myself and the horses.

Abandonment.

The desperation I feel to be seen consumes the space. I am

wounded – *no,* I am enough.

    I suddenly become aware of the tension in my body and adjust my feet, stretching my legs out and flipping the palms of my hands open. I don't need to live in a state of contraction, yearning to expand. I breathe into the sensation of the stretch, surrendering to length. Diva approaches from behind to support my full release.

Can I trust this?

    My mind wraps around this question and I hold it in my forehead, tensing my grip. *A cocoon.*

I'm safe.
Soften.
I am a mother
& a daughter.

    The sensation melts down my shoulders and cascades around my hips, flowing out the bottom of my feet before looping around to the center of my heart.

I am love.

    I allow that to spread, permeating through my body. Diva trails off, not staying longer than her support is needed. The wind whistles through the dirt, and I feel the coolness beneath my feet.

I wonder what it's like to be...

There's that yearning again – this is not presence. Time's up. I've got some work to do, and I'm enough.

I am.

sun-soaked shadows

I hold all these identities while searching for meaning within them. If everything was stripped away,
down to its essence –
the spirit within form –
what's left?

// the edge of identity

I am Hannah,
mother of August,
daughter of Karey,
grand-daughter of Janet & Annette,
great-granddaughter of Cora, Tillie,
Irene, Pearl.
Irish and Nordic bloodline
on stolen land.
forgotten ancestry,
a seed fallen from the stars.
time traveler
wearing time's scars.
descendant of the womb.
cosmic voyager
taking a stand.

mystified
& grounded.
curious & brave.
a paradox.
complexity
wrapped in a simple design.
so divine.

I am a river of love,
consciously removing debris
from impeding its flow.

I am.

// 1000 lifetimes healed

Our parents bury stories in our bones
with loving hands & lost dreams.
fertile soil,
soiled with stories of their own,
buried deeper than it seems.

We carry them like a birthright,
hold onto like a keepsake,
with all our might,
we hang tight –
hoarding stories
like they are something to lose.
Stowing stolen worries –
mementos like an altar of gold.

Before stories come to be,
they're first claimed, lived,
sometimes hidden –
like the body's personal mission.

A father's life of indecision
is a child's story of doubt
weaved together by guilt,
simply for existing,
taking up space,
& breathing all over the place.

a mother's escape from reality
is a story of abandonment,
a child's great search for God
in the eyes of another,

hannah alley

confusing love for neutrality
and running from lovers
if it goes deeper than sexuality.

just as stories are written in the sand,
they can be swept away by the sea,
the great remembrance
of all that's been
and could be.

sun-soaked shadows

how will i choose to spend this one precious day?
fully and completely present in my bones.
stretch when my body calls,
dance if it demands
and speak the truth when it rises in my throat.

this is it.

hannah alley

// becoming the one

when was the last time you were touched by the sun?
moved by the stars?
caressed by the moon?

we put so much emphasis
on finding 'the one' to complete us,
years searching for a lover
in white armor who can save us
the thrills, that endless rush.

instead i think i'll take communion with the breeze,
sleep under the stars for a while,
give my nervous system a restart
enter sacred union with the trees.

// who decides who is worthy of liberation?

today is the day she realized the root of all suffering is
to abandon the light of her soul for the false promise of
enlightenment, and to sacrifice the totality of this existence for
ownership of its individual parts.

liberation.
freedom.
sovereignty.

she wrapped her heart
in the web of her mind.
she believed power is given
and can be taken away,
rather than lived-in,
cherished everyday.

we allow fear
to burn in our bellies
while looking over our shoulders,
when we are the ones who lit the match.

rich with greed
for the right to air,
inhaling without gratitude
for the gift of breath.

it is all connected -
our longing for connection,
but our minds too twisted
to connect.

hannah alley

we are interconnected.
your sovereignty
emboldens my freedom,
and mine, yours.

i don't aim to skim over
the complexity of life, but
this is a declaration –

i am free.
you are free.
we are free.

so shoot bullets at our words
as they explode
off our hearts
and live on in our kin.
we'll continue to practice
the art of forgiveness.

liberation is oneness.
we are all it.
as sacred as the land.

Learning to Balance

I don't know how I can show my face at that yoga studio again. I can only imagine what they thought of the girl crying on her mat the entire time. It wasn't really a muffled cry either. There was sobbing. I could feel the instructor's concerned gaze, and while there was no judgment, I still felt like I was killing the vibe. I held it in as long as I could, really I did. Until I didn't. I just burst.

What did I expect? The last time I took Anton's class I was with her, and so to be back here, my first class since she died, I should have known this is more than my fragile heart can handle.

What are the odds that the sequencing would be similar? Maybe any sequence in that studio would feel familiar. One minute I'd be lengthening into triangle pose, and the next I'm remembering the way she wobbled on her mat next to me, barely keeping balance on two feet. I choke on my own laugher, and immediately I'm stabbed by guilt. *I shouldn't be laughing. I don't deserve to laugh. Besides, my laugh could never hold a match to hers.*

And this is when the tears start to flow.

When we took a pause in Balasana and he came over to me for an adjustment to deepen my pose, he didn't realize how much his hands were releasing what's been stuck in my hips. A whole lifetime of grief dripped off my bones with just one firm press on my lower back. He took a breath with me and as I exhaled, he pressed down and my knees widened as the weight I'd been carrying since birth resisted release. In the tension, I recalled a memory from our drive home, just months ago:

"*That was hard, I can't believe you do that everyday,*" she *said with wide eyes, searching mine. The way her mouth curves upward, I can see she's genuinely impressed, there's pride at the forefront of her words.*

"The way we show up on our mat is such a reflection for how we show up in life," I respond pointedly without making eye contact. There's a sharp undertone in my delivery that catches me off gaurd, "you should do it more," I add in, quickly, with a softer tone.

"Oh, I believe it." she confirmed, unbothered by my dig. I cringe at myself for how I treat her. I swear at that moment we were both remembering when she nearly fell over in a yogi squat. I steal a glance of her in the passenger seat looking ahead with sweat beaded on her forehead. She's never looked better, I think. I only wish I said it.

This is when I lose it. All the words I left unspoken. All the moments I allowed to float by. My hips crack open and love pours out onto the mat. Love floods the room and has nowhere to go. And I'm left in Child's Pose, drowning in memories. I'd give anything to go back to that moment. I'd hug her and tell her how much it meant to me that she came. That I have longed for this moment all my life, and even though I'm not showing it, my heart is swelling beyond measure.

The little girl inside me is pouring her tears onto this mat, yearning to be with her. I want this to become our thing. She could build her balance and reclaim her life. And then she'd be happy. I'd be whole again.

But she's not. And that's why I'm crying. Because she's gone, and I'm here on this mat balancing *just fine*.

//woman in waiting

there's a world inside
waiting to be explored
there's a woman inside
not to be ignored
she's the roaring fire
beneath a blanket of stars
the sweet whisper of trees
bringing the whole world
to its knees.
she's every heartbeat
every desire
all the women
you've ever admired.
she's the language
of a river
flowing under your skin
the perfect temperature
waiting for you to jump in.

hannah alley

// balancing act

at this point,
i know i couldn't have
experienced this the way i did
without first experiencing the
exact opposite.
my reactions were projections
of all the polarized pieces
within myself, scrambling for
harmony,
creating dis-ease.
living in the outliers
of my own dual nature
or sliding between extremes.

here i am,
a balancing act
dancing between worlds.

sun-soaked shadows

the bees lured me in,
deeper into the vibrations
of the forest.

a lesson awaits.

i've tasted death.

in its sweet darkness,
the veil between worlds
lifted
and all its mystery
lost
in the blinding sunlight.

i touched the stars at midnight.

//character development

She was wild. not altogether feral, but unrefined. There was much of her that this world's conditioning couldn't, and never did, touch. Her legs went unshaven, hair uncombed, and without any real reason to obey the law. And still, the purity of her heart was primal, to trust others was just her nature. She held no grudges and was forgiving to a fault. When something was funny, she didn't hold back. All of herself was revealed in her laugh, the way her head would pull back with neck outstretched, and her shoulders bounced as the lines in her forehead deepened... she took everyone for a ride through the canyons of her soul. In the tragedy where her story ends, Karey handed us a pile of lessons for how to live unruly.

Someday I'll share them. I'm still sifting through.

// remembering who i am

coming home,
planting new seeds
putting to rest the 'would have'
& 'what could be.'

releasing the past.
letting it be, to finally allow
all the good things
that were always meant for me.

shedding my armor,
putting down my shield
because to love & be loved
is my life's greatest honor.

and i've loved, far & wide
and i haven't stopped –
now there's the problem, you see,
i've not even tried to let go,
respect the flow & ride the tide.

all the doors
i've wanted closed
stay open,
only a crack,
just in case anyone
decides to come back.

and some do, so i smile
happy to paint all the blue times gold
convinced this is what i've been unable to find,
not paying no mind to the mold

hannah alley

growing inside
i choose to ignorantly ignore
this pattern i've repeated
again and again
is a twisted game i play –
where i'm always left defeated
but who's keeping score?

i'm over it, i'm not having fun
like my whole life i've been on the run.

but not anymore.
i see clearly what i'm chasing
memories
my mind keeps erasing
the pain of losing you
again, and again
the golden ray...
life painted blue.

as much as i try,
lord knows i do
no matter how many times i try & change it
the truth always remains true –
you left,
then you died
& no one can ever replace you.

even though i've tried to collect lovers
just to prove i am lovable
taking the path backwards
won't rewind time
that's the grieving man's mind.

the only way out is through
stop running

sun-soaked shadows

& numbing
the hour is time to heal
core wounds
created in the womb
felt in my womb
a yearning to be loved
first felt growing inside you.

patterns imprinted
from mother to daughter
two runaways
on a runaway train
lost in life's sonder.

to abandon myself
is to turn my back on you.

a fool on the edge of a cliff
holding the world in her womb
is a woman remembering
wide-eyed with wisdom
she caught
the midnight train to everywhere.

and this train
this one's right on track...

hannah alley

// Dave Matthews was right

I felt her today
in the solitude of my womb
her silence was wisdom
found in the space between
each breath.

//what it does

grief picks you right off the ground
shakes you to your core
and bends you without mercy.
it empties you,
spilling out everything that's ever been kept inside
for you to face,
search through,
remember
and discover.

grief consumes
and takes you on a ride
to the darkside
that lives deep inside.

grief will steal your last breath
but despite death's whisper,
you'll inhale it all in,
and stretch wider,
until you transform –
and transform it,
until
the cord snaps
and blood drains to white knuckles.
what you've been holding
with all your might,
gone.
and just after it kills you,
                            light.

and standing in the ashes of despair,

hannah alley

you put yourself back together,
brick by brick
and remember.

its same same,
but different.
always
different.
never the same.

On Choosing Life

"I am no longer in control of where I place my feet, the island is being revealed to me, I am being propelled along its path, finding things I have never even thought or dreamed of."

– Paulo Coelho, *The Zahir*

I used to say, convincingly, *I don't want kids.*

The truth is, oftentimes I feel unlovable. This has followed me through the years, casting a shadow over friendships, plaguing relationships and destroying my sense of self-worth. I was afraid a child would only validate this story that lived rent-free in my body. Everyone I have ever loved has proven me unlovable, unworthy of sticking around. Surely the pure eyes of a child would see right through to my dark core and reject me too.

Because of this, when I found out I was pregnant, one of my first calls was to an abortion clinic. By coincidence (divine intervention) it was too early and they couldn't confirm I was pregnant. My son's claim to life was undetected by everyone except me. They couldn't legally offer me any medication to make it all go away, and told me to reschedule an appointment in a week. I was forced to sit with myself.

I went home and spent that tempered May afternoon sitting on my patio with Paulo Coelho. Lost, I read, *"I am no longer in control of where I place my feet, the island is being revealed to me, I am being propelled along its path, finding things I have never even thought or dreamed of."*

In that moment, tears flooded my eyes, the wind swept the sweetest melody through the trees and deep in the shadows of my soul, I felt a whisper of light. For the first time, I think in my life, I heard God loud & clear. I was being told to surrender control and let my heart lead me down an unknown path, into the great mystery of life. Unsure of the journey ahead, I knew it was the way home.

Sometimes the very thing we need to confront our deepest fears is everything which we push away. In that moment, I vowed to follow those whispers and let the cascading river of love flow freely. And so I did.

My son was a homecoming to the purest love I had ever known. *The love a mother has for her child is holy.*

When I told my mother the news, she was overjoyed. She smiled with a pride I hadn't seen before, like a remembering of when she, too, carried life inside her womb. Then, she congratulated me on finally becoming a woman. As a self-identified feminist, I was offended. Was I not a woman before? Am I not a woman now?

Years later, I think about my reaction and lack of compassion or curiosity behind her statement. I wish I had asked her. Yet, as I sit here and reflect on it all, *I think I get it.* I can feel into the intention behind her words and find resonance. Through motherhood I discovered a wider version of myself as a woman and more intimately learned to define what womanhood means *for me*. I was a woman and a mother. Becoming a mother allowed me to see my womanhood from an entirely new vantage point and my reality shifted drastically. The Fool becoming the World in the end.

Being pregnant was like standing on the edge of a dense forest. It's impossible to see through the lush landscape. I had no idea what I would find as I stepped beyond the edges of where I felt safe. Motherhood was the unknown and I was within my range of knowing as a woman. Before I entered the birth portal, forging my own path through the tall grass, I thought I knew about love and life. I was so certain. With that came self-righteousness.

I arrived in motherhood like I arrived in nature, *humbled with moss-stained knees.* The woman I was, shaped by tales I was told, stories inherited and the narratives I tried on as a young girl needed to shed for the mother to rise. My hips had moved mountains. My body had opened and brought life into this world. I was changed, discovering things of myself I had never even thought or dreamed of. I met my most powerful self when I became a mother, and it's been guiding how I show up as a woman ever since.

When August chose me, I started the winding journey of unfolding and am learning how to choose life fully and wholeheartedly each day. Motherhood has emboldened the whole woman who always lived within, and continues to offer the most potent lessons on how to live.

Thanks, mom, for the reflection in the afterlife.

hannah alley

I arrived
in motherhood
like
I arrived in nature:
humbled,
with moss-stained knees.

// rediscovering love after loss

a life of adventure
slow dance,
and some sweet romance
cooking dinner kind of night.

spontaneity beneath our feet
because as long as we're together...
yeah, life is sweet.

a soul with the courage to expand into the man you
want to be –
and the openness to be loved by a woman.

a tender heart.
firm hands
to feel into my energy
and sip it slow –
let's take our time
like a sweet sway with the divine.

your eyes rain down on me
attention is affection
and it fills my cup.
days in the sun
are my kind of fun.

hannah alley

all we know
everything we thought
burns in the sun
in the name of metamorphosis.

from ash we rise,
and that's how we get our wings.

// 2.2.22

and he waited
patiently waited for her to take flight,
to fly toward the dreams alive in her bones.
tangled in her past,
fear tugged at her mind
freezing the fire that lights her heart.

unwinding the web
rethreading new stories
he did what he could to ensure a safe flight
but knew the first lift off had to be hers.

as soon as she opened her heart to the wind
all of her dreams flowed
in the river of time
and she stepped in, to claim her win.

truth is in the do –
and that's how she learned to fly.

hannah alley

// Aquarius

to know her
is to dance + have fun.
to feel her
is to stand in the sun.

love flows
with innate curiosity
like a wildly free,
sweet melody.

heart as open
as the shape of the wind.
she simply desires
us all to win.

style
class
her inner fire burns
like sweet grass.

a copper heart
with a garnet soul,
in a friend
you'll never want more.

sweet child,
you're a star
one of a kind
simply divine.

// one in the same

all life is connected and moves in cycles
unending circles
the seasons move in a circle,
as do the sun and moon and stars and earth.
nothing truly ends, but just begins anew again.

we are of the earth,
the sea,
and the sun.
made of the wind,
clouds and stone,
and of spirit and light.

death initiates purification
which inspires seasons of bloom.
circles and cycles,
synced and choreographed.

hannah alley

your love is a river in the sky
your eyes are the sun
slipping beneath
silky darkness.

...the news of Alliance is being acquired, and ...feeling resistant to jumping back in after ...asting the slow down. The frustration — or pressure ...s been building and August's begging for ...y attention while mine was focused on ...rk sent me over the edge into that dark ...nnel of boiling water & I screamed. My ...tbursts are becoming less extreme, shorter ...d further apart as I expand my ...emotional container — but it doesn't ...ake it feel any better. I won't punish myself ...r it, but I do worry the imprint I leave ...n August. Sometimes, because the lid blows ...o suddenly, there's a shock that sets in on ...is face, immediately followed by tears. ...nd I know I've hurt his core. It's the ...nowing of this that brings my temperature ...own and I take a few minutes to myself, ...ollecting composure & reclaiming my breath ...efore knocking on his door, which he now locks ... keep me out. Sometimes he'll let me in ...and we talk — recounting what happened & ...aring our feelings but othertimes he yells ..."go away" and I know he needs to process ...ome more, so I wait for him to call my name ...d try not to punish myself.

...ast night after a few games of war ...a story read a guided meditation, ...gust was ½ sleeping, nuzzled up underneath ...neck, under my chin and he asked, ...o you not care about me anymore?"

hannah alley

// august wisdom

"mom, it's ok! it doesn't matter if they say it better than what you say. it matters that it comes from your heart."

so, i should get out of my head and into my heart?

"exactly...
...I love you, mom."

and those are the sweetest words my ears have ever heard.

//*sun-soaked shadows*

the sunlight cascading through the shadows of time
is my mind releasing the past.
there's no need to rewind,
the present is sweet
and warm.
the sun radiates behind me –
          a flicker within.
               i feel at home in my skin
                   and this...
                      this is where my story begins.

       i can hear the wind, again.
            forgiven of my sins,
i think i can finally live, again,
          free as the wind.
stretching across the bedroom floor,
i am the light,
        and the door that opens
               to a life of so much more.
                   i'm here to fly,
                       and fly high i will.

                            my will is strong
                   because i trust the divine
         and my place *here* across space and time.

      she chose me
   and i her

she gave me sight
when she said goodnight.

hannah alley

afraid of the dark hallways in my mind,
so i swallowed the void
ate the pain i was trying to hide
only to find…
         the room exploded with light.

                  my invitation to embrace
              the pain i thought defined me.
*   i think i love these sun-soaked shadows.*
*   they awoke the poet inside me.*

thank you

hannah alley is a entrepreneur, doula and birth educator living on the ancestral lands of the Akimel O'odham, the original stewards of present-day Phoenix with her partner and their son. While she has been writing all her life as a healing practice, poetry has opened doors for deeper self-discovery and creativity. Her mission is to share how loss can open us to the most tender love of life, if we allow it.

She published her first children's book *everywhere, and in my heart* in 2019, which was inspired by a poem she wrote after losing her mom.

This is her debut poetry collection.

Made in the USA
Columbia, SC
02 October 2024